THE LEGENDARY SONGS OF

Don McLean

ISBN 978-1-4234-3623-2

7777 W. BLUEMOUND RD. P.O. BOX 13819 MILWAUKEE, WI 53213

For all works contained herein:
Unauthorized copying, arranging, adapting, recording or public performance is an infringement of copyright.
Infringers are liable under the law.

Visit Hal Leonard Online at
www.halleonard.com

Don McLean was born on October 2nd 1945 in New Rochelle, NY to Elizabeth and Donald McLean. By the age of five he had developed an interest in all forms of music and would spend hours listening to the radio and 78rpm records. As a teenager, he purchased his first guitar and took opera lessons paid for by his sister. Don's musical focus was very much on folk, thanks (in part) to The Weavers landmark 1955 recording "Live at Carnegie Hall". Don was determined to become a professional musician and singer and, as a 16 year old, he was already making contacts in the business.

In 1963, while at Villanova University, Don met and became friends with Jim Croce. Don recorded his first studio sessions in 1964 and 1965, and was invited to join an offshoot of the Rooftop Singers. However, even at that time, Don saw himself as a troubadour and turned down the offer. After leaving Villanova, there was a six year period during which time Don performed throughout New York and New England. He appeared with such artists as Blood, Sweat, and Tears, the James Gang, Herbie Mann, Brownie McGee and Sonny Terry, Melanie, Steppenwolf, Arlo Guthrie, Pete Seeger, Janis Ian, Josh White, Ten Wheel Drive and others. This was the start of Don McLean's career as a professional singer, songwriter, musician and performer, and was further aided by his signing with the William Morris Agency in 1969. Don recorded his first album, "Tapestry", in Berkeley, CA, with the student riots going on outside the studio door while Don was singing "And I Love You So" inside.

The transition to major international stardom began in 1971 with the release of "American Pie," recorded on May 26th, 1971, and receiving it's first radio airplay one month later. Thirty years later, "American Pie" was voted number 5 in a poll of the 365 "Songs of the Century" compiled by the Recording Industry Association of America and the National Endowment for the Arts. The top five were: "Over the Rainbow" by Judy Garland; "White Christmas" by Bing Crosby; "This Land Is Your Land" by Woody Guthrie; "Respect" by Aretha Franklin; and "American Pie" by Don McLean. "American Pie" was issued as a double A-side single in November 1971 and charted within a month. The second single, "Vincent", charted on March 18th, 1972. The "American Pie" album remained at #1 in the UK for 7 weeks in 1972, and in the UK charts for 53 consecutive weeks.

In the wake of "American Pie", Don became a major concert attraction and was able to call upon material not only from his two albums but from a tremendous repertoire of old concert hall numbers and the complete catalogues of singers such as Buddy Holly, and another McLean influence, Frank Sinatra. The years spent playing gigs in small clubs and coffee houses paid off with well-paced performances. Don's first concert at the Albert Hall in 1972 was a triumphant success, he played there many more times, and sold out the venue once again in October of 2007.

With all this success, "Tapestry" was reissued by United Artists and charted in the USA on 12th February 1972 reaching #111 and the top-15 in the United Kingdom; it includes two of Don's most famous songs: "And I Love You So" and "Castles in the Air". Don's third album, simply entitled "Don McLean", included the song "The Pride Parade" that provides an insight into Don's immediate reaction to his instant superstardom. The album also contained the charting records "Dreidel" and "If We Try," which are included here. The fourth album, "Playin Favourites" became a top-40 hit in the UK in 1973. The album included a rendition of Buddy Holly's "Everyday", which returned Don to the UK singles chart. 1973 was also a great success for Don McLean the

songwriter and Don McLean the performer. Perry Como recorded "And I Love You So" from the "Tapestry" album and took it to the UK top-5 and American top-30. Como's version was nominated for a Grammy but was beaten by a song about Don, "Killing Me Softly With His Song", sung by Roberta Flack (and written by Norman Gimbel and Charles Fox after Lori Leiberman had attended a McLean concert at the LA Troubadour).

Throughout the 1970s, Don McLean remained an in-demand concert performer. In 1975, 85000 fans attended his London Hyde Park concert. 1977 gave us the "Prime Time" album before, in 1978, Don would work with many of Elvis Presley's old musicians. The result was "Chain Lightning." The early 1980s saw further chart success with a new recording of "Castles in the Air" and the #3 recording of "Crying", which was also #1 around the world with Roy Orbison's version, which re-ignited Roy's career. Some people are amazed when they read how successful, Don McLean has been. Far from fading away (like some of his 1970s singer-songwriter contemporaries), Don has remained very much in the upper echelons of popular music.

Don remained busy in the 1990's, and a favourite memory for many fans is Don performing "American Pie" live on "Top of the Pops" in 1991. In 1995, the band Guns N' Roses took a replica of Don's version of "Since I Don't Have You" (a US top-20 hit for Don in April 1981) to the UK top-10, which was followed by "American Pie" returning to the top-40 charts with a techno version performed by European artist, Just Luis. The Fugees cover of "Killing Me Softly With His Song", was one of the biggest selling singles of the 1996, and in 1997 Don joined Garth Brooks on stage at his Central Park concert (attended by over 500,000 people) to perform "American Pie" and ignite his third career comeback. According to Don, his first "comeback" had been the release of "Vincent" and the second, the release and massive success of "Crying". Two years later Garth Brooks repaid the favour by appearing as a special guest (with Nanci Griffith) on Don's first ever American TV special, broadcast on PBS and now available as the "Starry Starry Night" video, DVD and CD. A month later, Don McLean wound up the 20th century by performing "American Pie" for President Clinton at the Lincoln Memorial Gala In Washington D.C.

In 2000, Madonna recorded a cover version of "American Pie" that upon release in the UK entered the official singles chart at number 1 and made the US top-30 on air play points alone. Even more surprising than Madonna having a hit with a Don McLean song, was George Michael's decision in 2003 to record "The Grave", from the "American Pie" album, as a protest against the Iraq war. He recorded the song for MTV and performed it live on Top of the Pops.

The 21st Century has seen a number of new honors for Don McLean and his music. Iona College conferred an honorary doctorate on Don in 2001 and, in February 2002, "American Pie" was finally inducted into the Grammy Hall of Fame. In 2004 Don McLean was inaugurated into the National Academy of Popular Music Songwriters' Hall of Fame. The ceremony took place on June 10th, 2004 in New York City and Don's award was presented by Garth Brooks, who paid a glowing tribute.

In 2007 Don shared his professional life story in Alan Howard's biography, "The Don McLean Story: Killing Us Softly With His Songs," and hit the international charts with the CD/DVD issue, "The Legendary Don McLean." In 2008 a new exhibition debuted on Las Vegas' renowned Fremont Street entitled "Don McLean's American Pie," paying tribute to his music with the nightly light spectacle and featuring videos and representations of his songs. Today, Don continues to be a busy and in demand performer, and as of 2008, he completed yet another world-wide tour. As we approach the end of the first decade of the millennium, Don McLean doesn't show any signs of slowing down.

4   *American Pie*

14   *And I Love You So*

18   *Bad Girl*

28   *Birthday Song*

34   *Bronco Bill's Lament*

23   *Castles in the Air*

40   *Crossroads*

44   *Dreidel*

62   *Empty Chairs*

66   *Everybody Loves Me, Baby*

70   *If We Try*

76   *La La Love You*

84   *The Legend of Andrew McCrew*

51   *Magdalene Lane*

92   *The More You Pay, The More It's Worth*

97   *Orphans of Wealth*

102   *Pride Parade*

108   *Respectable*

114   *Tapestry*

124   *Three Flights Up*

134   *Till Tomorrow*

117   *To Have and to Hold*

138   *Vincent (Starry Starry Night)*

148   *Winter Has Me in Its Grip*

143   *Winterwood*

158   *Wonderful Baby*

152   *You Have Lived*

AMERICAN PIE

Words and Music by
DON McLEAN

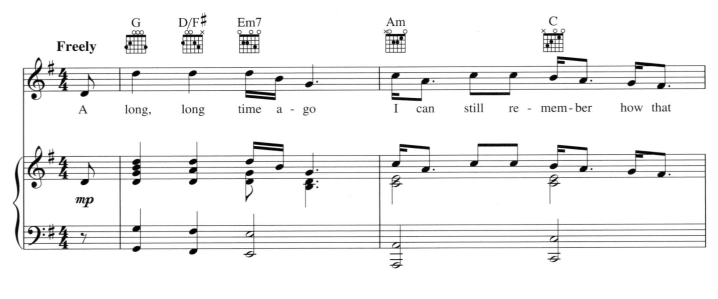

A long, long time a- go I can still re- mem- ber how that

mu- sic used to make me smile. _____ And

I knew if I had my chance that I could make those peo- ple dance and

Copyright © 1971, 1972 BENNY BIRD CO., INC.
Copyright Renewed
All Rights Controlled and Administered by SONGS OF UNIVERSAL, INC.
All Rights Reserved   Used by Permission

Additional Lyrics

2. Now for ten years we've been on our own,
   And moss grows fat on a rollin' stone
   But that's not how it used to be
   When the jester sang for the king and queen
   In a coat he borrowed from James Dean
   And a voice that came from you and me
   Oh and while the king was looking down,
   The jester stole his thorny crown
   The courtroom was adjourned,
   No verdict was returned
   And while Lenin read a book on Marx
   The quartet practiced in the park
   And we sang dirges in the dark
   The day the music died
   We were singin'...bye-bye...etc.

3. Helter-skelter in the summer swelter
   The birds flew off with a fallout shelter
   Eight miles high and fallin' fast,
   It landed foul on the grass
   The players tried for a forward pass,
   With the jester on the sidelines in a cast
   Now the half-time air was sweet perfume
   While the sergeants played a marching tune
   We all got up to dance
   But we never got the chance
   'Cause the players tried to take the field,
   The marching band refused to yield
   Do you recall what was revealed
   The day the music died
   We started singin'... bye-bye...etc.

4. And there we were all in one place,
   A generation lost in space
   With no time left to start again
   So come on, Jack be nimble, Jack be quick,
   Jack Flash sat on a candlestick
   'Cause fire is the devil's only friend
   And as I watched him on the stage
   My hands were clenched in fits of rage
   No angel born in hell
   Could break that Satan's spell
   And as the flames climbed high into the night
   To light the sacrificial rite
   I saw Satan laughing with delight
   The day the music died
   He was singin'...bye-bye...etc.

AND I LOVE YOU SO

Words and Music by
DON McLEAN

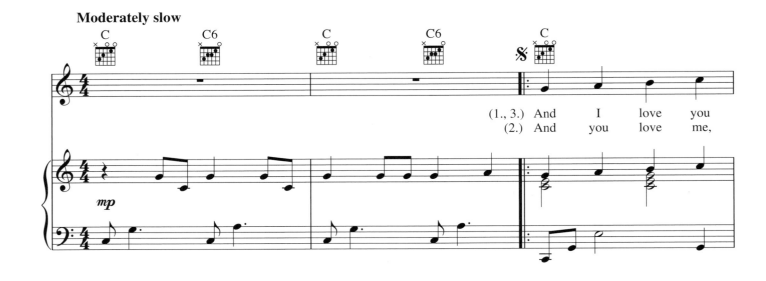

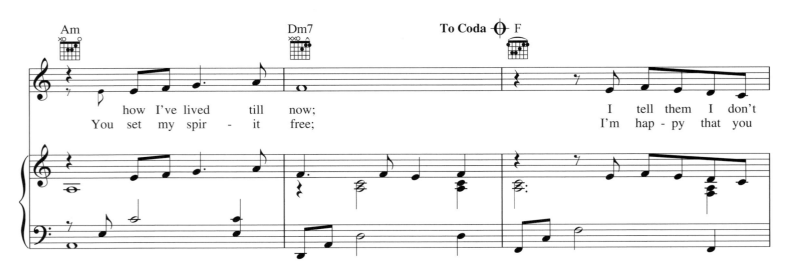

Copyright © 1970, 1972 BENNY BIRD CO., INC.
Copyright Renewed
All Rights Controlled and Administered by SONGS OF UNIVERSAL, INC.
All Rights Reserved   Used by Permission

BAD GIRL

Words and Music by
DON McLEAN

'Round and 'round, the years go 'round and 'round, and man-y a dream is lost in the nas-ty cit-y sound.

Fast Shuffle tempo

Copyright © 1970 BENNY BIRD CO., INC.
Copyright Renewed
All Rights Controlled and Administered by SONGS OF UNIVERSAL, INC.
All Rights Reserved   Used by Permission

found a lit-tle pad in a bad ____ neigh-bor-hood; _ She learned a-bout life and it was

quite a shock, but now she knocks them down with the best on the block. _

(Spoken:) "Yeah, and that's really a shame too, because she was her daddy's pride and joy."

rit.

CASTLES IN THE AIR

Words and Music by
DON McLEAN

Copyright © 1969, 1972 BENNY BIRD CO., INC.
Copyright Renewed
All Rights Controlled and Administered by SONGS OF UNIVERSAL, INC.
All Rights Reserved   Used by Permission

BIRTHDAY SONG

Words and Music by
DON McLEAN

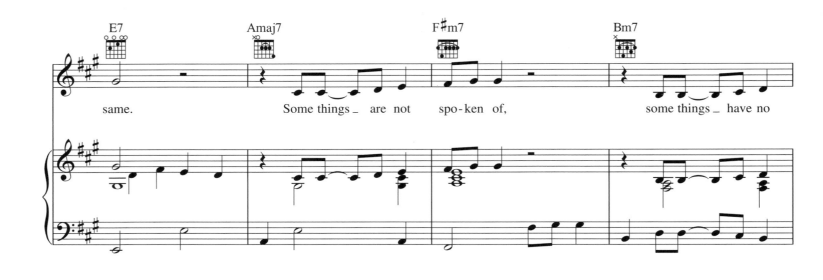

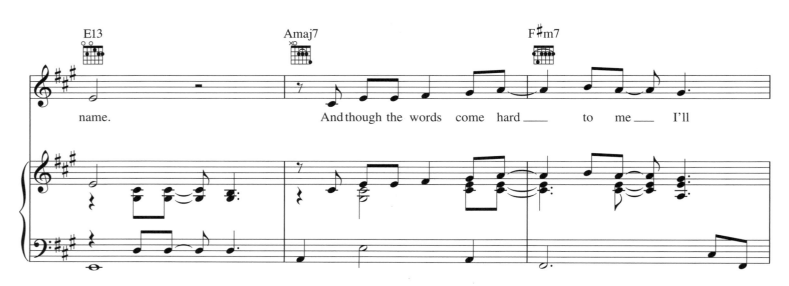

Copyright © 1972 BENNY BIRD CO., INC.
Copyright Renewed
All Rights Controlled and Administered by SONGS OF UNIVERSAL, INC.
All Rights Reserved   Used by Permission

BRONCO BILL'S LAMENT

Words and Music by
DON McLEAN

Copyright © 1972 BENNY BIRD CO., INC.
Copyright Renewed
All Rights Controlled and Administered by SONGS OF UNIVERSAL, INC.
All Rights Reserved   Used by Permission

CROSSROADS

Words and Music by
DON McLEAN

I've got noth-ing on my mind, noth-ing to re-
Can you re-mem-ber who I was, can you still

mem-ber, Noth-ing to for-get, And I've got
feel it? Can you find my pain?

noth-ing __ to re-gret. But I'm all tied up on the
Can you heal it? Then lay your hands up-on me

Copyright © 1971, 1973 BENNY BIRD CO., INC.
Copyrights Renewed
All Rights Controlled and Administered by SONGS OF UNIVERSAL, INC.
All Rights Reserved   Used by Permission

DREIDEL

Words and Music by
DON McLEAN

Copyright © 1972 BENNY BIRD CO., INC.
Copyright Renewed
All Rights Controlled and Administered by SONGS OF UNIVERSAL, INC.
All Rights Reserved   Used by Permission

MAGDALENE LANE

Words and Music by
DON McLEAN

Copyright © 1971 BENNY BIRD CO., INC.
Copyright Renewed
All Rights Controlled and Administered by SONGS OF UNIVERSAL, INC.
All Rights Reserved   Used by Permission

M. G. M. Stu - di - os can't make the nut, They're
Proph - et has come to the king - dom of lights, but there's

auc - tion - ing Dor - o - thy's shoes; _____
no one to lis - ten or learn; _____ And the

Ga - ble is gone, the Good Witch is a slut, And
Sav - ior per - forms for the Proph - et's de - light, While dis -

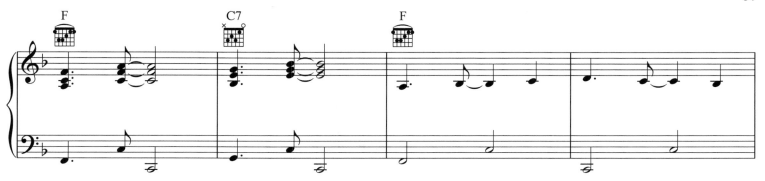

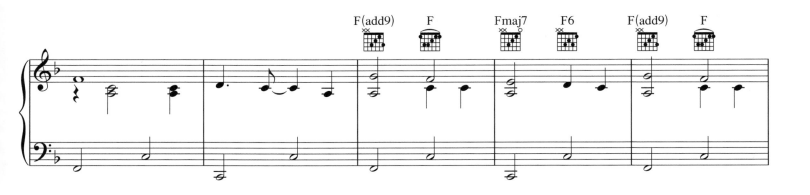

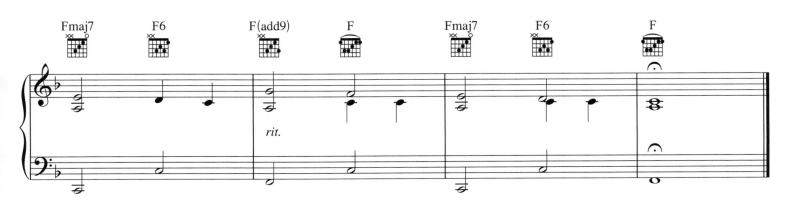

EMPTY CHAIRS

Words and Music by
DON McLEAN

Copyright © 1971 BENNY BIRD CO., INC.
Copyright Renewed
All Rights Controlled and Administered by SONGS OF UNIVERSAL, INC.
All Rights Reserved   Used by Permission

EVERYBODY LOVES ME, BABY

Words and Music by
DON McLEAN

Copyright © 1971, 1973 BENNY BIRD CO., INC.
Copyright Renewed
All Rights Controlled and Administered by SONGS OF UNIVERSAL, INC.
All Rights Reserved Used by Permission

Additional Lyrics

2. The purist race I've bred for thee,
   To live in my democracy;
   The highest human pedigree awaits your
   First born boy baby.

   My face on every coin engraved,
   The anarchists are all enslaved;
   My own flag is forever waved
   By the grateful people I have saved.
   You see, *(Chorus)*

3. No land is beyond my claim,
   When land is seized in the people's name;
   By evil men who rob and maim,
   If war is hell, I'm not to blame.

   Why you can't blame me, I'm Heaven's child,
   I'm the second son of Mary mild;
   And twice removed from Oscar Wilde,
   But he didn't mind, why he just smiled.
   You see, *(Chorus)*

4. Now the ocean parts when I walk through,
   The clouds dissolve, the sky turns blue;
   I'm held in very great value by
   Everyone I meet but you.

   'Cause I've used my talents as I could,
   I've done some bad, I've done some good;
   I did a whole lot better than they thought I could,
   So come on and treat me like you should.
   Because *(Chorus)*

IF WE TRY

Words and Music by
DON McLEAN

When I ___ see ___ you on ___ the street, ___ I

lose my con - cen - tra - tion. Just the thought ___ that we ___

___ might meet ___ cre - ates an - ti - ci - pa - tion. Won't you

Copyright © 1972 BENNY BIRD CO., INC.
Copyright Renewed
All Rights Controlled and Administered by SONGS OF UNIVERSAL, INC.
All Rights Reserved   Used by Permission

LA LA LOVE YOU

Words and Music by
DON McLEAN

Copyright © 1973 BENNY BIRD CO., INC.
Copyright Renewed
All Rights Controlled and Administered by SONGS OF UNIVERSAL, INC.
All Rights Reserved   Used by Permission

grow-ing   to keep you sat - is - fied ___   and if you

keep your green ___ light show - ing   well, you can take me ___ for a ride. ___

___   'Cause I   la la la la la la love ___

your lo - co - mo - tion show, ___ 'cause my

driv - ing wheel ___ is driv - ing and my pis - ton's work - ing good. ___

___ And if your mo - tor gives ___ you some trou - ble, ba - by, I'll take a

look un - der - neath your hood. ___ *(Yes, I would.)* 'Cause I

D.S. al Coda

So if you want to make me hap - py ____ here is all you got - ta do; ____ Just let ____ me ride ____ your box -

THE LEGEND OF ANDREW McCREW

Words and Music by
DON McLEAN

Copyright © 1974 BENNY BIRD CO., INC.
Copyright Renewed
All Rights Controlled and Administered by SONGS OF UNIVERSAL, INC.
All Rights Reserved   Used by Permission

THE MORE YOU PAY,
The More It's Worth

Words and Music by
DON McLEAN

The auc-tion-eer said, _____ "I'm not through _

_ yet. Here's a horse the likes of which you've _ nev-er seen." And the

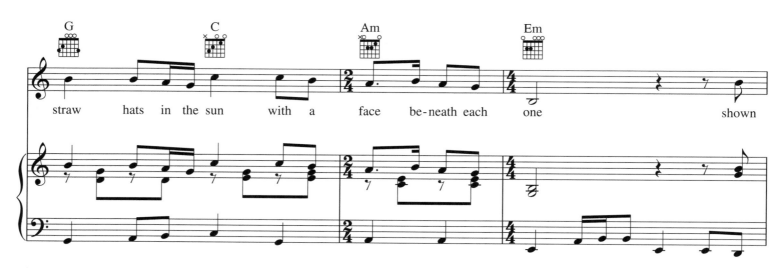

straw hats in the sun with a face be-neath each one shown

Copyright © 1972 BENNY BIRD CO., INC.
Copyright Renewed
All Rights Controlled and Administered by SONGS OF UNIVERSAL, INC.
All Rights Reserved   Used by Permission

doubt-ful and the auc-tion-eer __ got __ mean. Do you think that you can find a horse like

this ev-'ry day? I don't think there's an-y bet-ter on this earth and the more you

pay, the more it's worth. Then out she

came, _____ a snow-white __ mare,
hung _____ with emp-ty __ blues.

ORPHANS OF WEALTH

Words and Music by
DON McLEAN

Copyrig © 1970 BENNY BIRD CO., INC.
Copyright Renewed
All Rights Controlled and Administered by SONGS OF UNIVERSAL, INC.
All Rights Reserved   Used by Permission

floods in the nurs-'ry and a child ___ is cry - ing. He's hun - gry and

cold. _____ His life has been sold. His young face looks old. ___ It's the

face of A - mer - i - ca dy - ing.

Additional Lyrics

5. And with roaches and rickets and rats in the thickets
   Infested diseased and decaying
   With rags and no shoes and skin sores that ooze
   By the poisonous pools they are playing

6. In shacks of two rooms that are rotting wood tombs
   With corpses breathing inside them
   And we pity their plight as they call in the night
   And we do all that we can to hide them.
   Chorus

PRIDE PARADE

Words and Music by
DON McLEAN

It start-ed out quite sim-ply as com-plex things can
And soon you have suc-cumbed to what the oth-ers all be-
are sure-ly just as e-vil as the worst my tongue can

Copyright © 1972 BENNY BIRD CO., INC.
Copyright Renewed
All Rights Controlled and Administered by SONGS OF UNIVERSAL, INC.
All Rights Reserved   Used by Permission

days.

RESPECTABLE

Words and Music by
DON McLEAN

Oh, it ain't so eas - y, is ___ it? You al - most lost your
cor - dial - ly they caught you and they asked you to o - bey ___

place. And per - haps you're won - der - ing how you're going to
___ and they threw you in - to pri - son just in

cope with your dis - grace.
case you could not pay.

Well, your wealth is well es - tab -
Well, King Ar - thur joust - ed

Copyright © 1971 BENNY BIRD CO., INC.
Copyright Renewed
All Rights Controlled and Administered by SONGS OF UNIVERSAL, INC.
All Rights Reserved Used by Permission

TAPESTRY

Words and Music by
DON McLEAN

Copyright © 1970 BENNY BIRD CO., INC.
Copyright Renewed
All Rights Controlled and Administered by SONGS OF UNIVERSAL, INC.
All Rights Reserved   Used by Permission

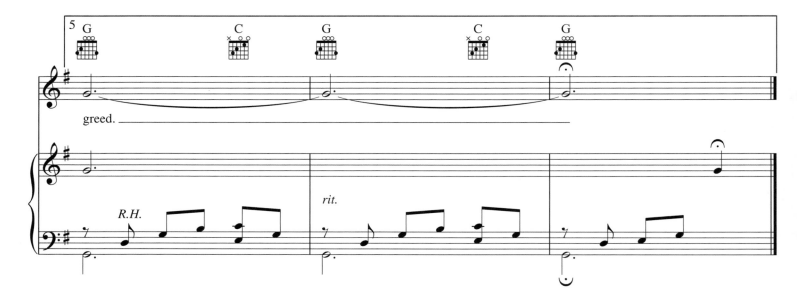

greed.

Additional Lyrics

2. Every breeze that blows kindly is one crystal breath,
   We exhale on the blue diamond heaven;
   As gentle to touch as the hands of the healer,
   As soft as farewells whispered over the coffin,
   We're poisoned by venom with each breath we take,
   From the brown sulphur chimney
   And the black highway snake.

3. Every dawn that breaks golden is held in suspension,
   Like the yolk of the egg in albumen;
   Where the birth and the death of unseen generations,
   Are interdependent in vast orchestration,
   And painted in colors of tapestry thread,
   When the dying are born and the living are dead.

4. Every pulse of your heartbeat is one liquid moment,
   That flows through the veins of your being;
   Like a river of life flowing on since creation,
   Approaching the sea with each new generation,
   You're now just a stagnant and rancid disgrace,
   That is rapidly drowning the whole human race.

5. Every fish that swims silent, every bird that flies freely,
   Every doe that steps softly;
   Every crisp leaf that falls, all the flowers that grow,
   On this colorful tapestry, somehow they know,
   That if man is allowed to destroy all we need,
   He will soon have to pay with his life
   For his greed.

TO HAVE AND TO HOLD

Words and Music by
DON McLEAN

Slow Waltz

As the sea - sons go ____

cir - cling, ___ and the years _____ spin a -
chil - dren or live _____ all a -

way, and the high - way grows
lone, the light of our

Copyright © 1987 DON McLEAN MUSIC
All Rights Controlled and Administered by SONGS OF UNIVERSAL, INC.
All Rights Reserved   Used by Permission

THREE FLIGHTS UP

Words and Music by
DON McLEAN

Copyright © 1970 BENNY BIRD CO., INC.
Copyright Renewed
All Rights Controlled and Administered by SONGS OF UNIVERSAL, INC.
All Rights Reserved   Used by Permission

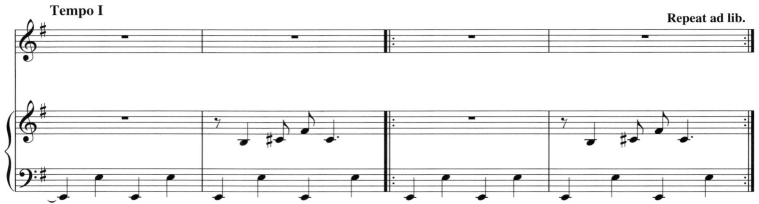

TILL TOMORROW

Words and Music by
DON McLEAN

Slowly

What can this be, can you tell me? _____ Would you like to dis-cov-er why we're not free to be lov-ers? _____ I've been want-ing to ask __ you,

Copyright © 1971, 1973 BENNY BIRD CO., INC.
Copyrights Renewed
All Rights Controlled and Administered by SONGS OF UNIVERSAL, INC.
All Rights Reserved   Used by Permission

VINCENT
(Starry Starry Night)

Words and Music by
DON McLEAN

Copyright © 1971, 1972 BENNY BIRD CO., INC.
Copyrights Renewed
All Rights Controlled and Administered by SONGS OF UNIVERSAL, INC.
All Rights Reserved   Used by Permission

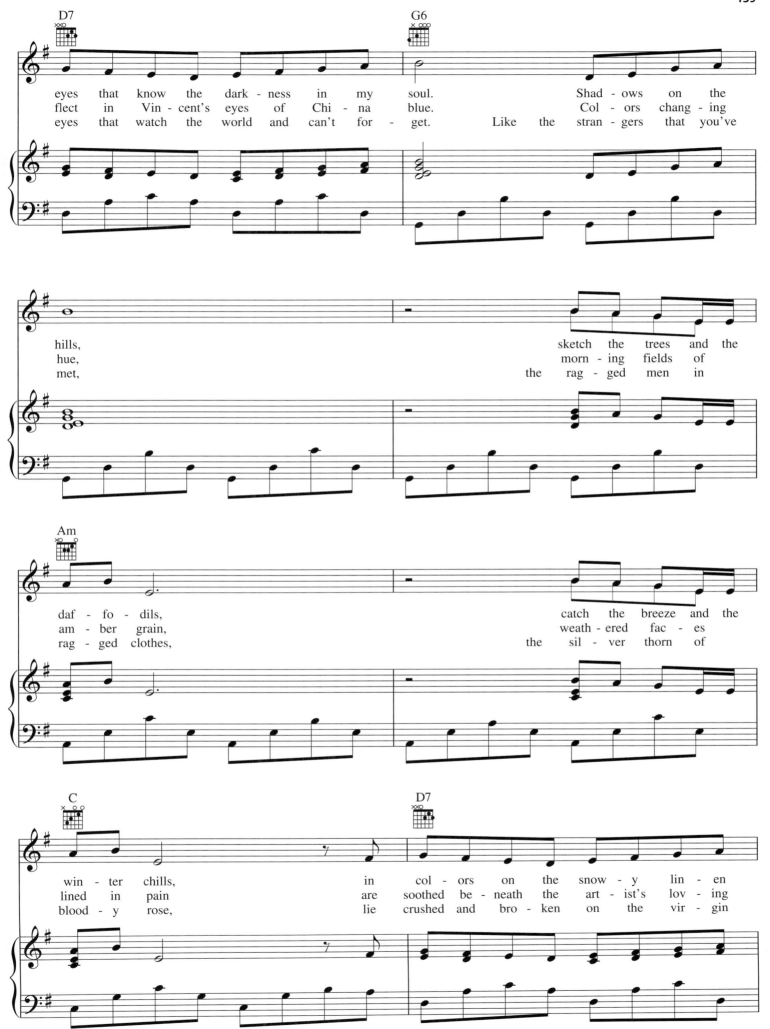

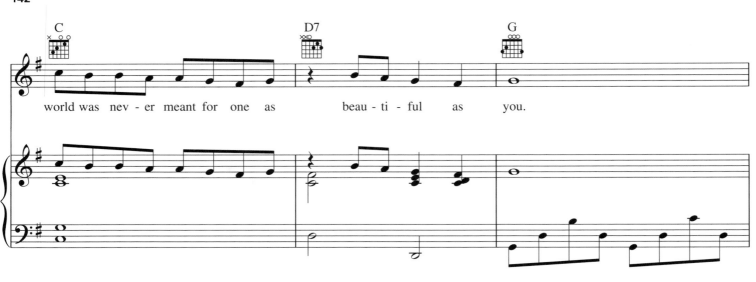

world was nev - er meant for one as beau - ti - ful as you.

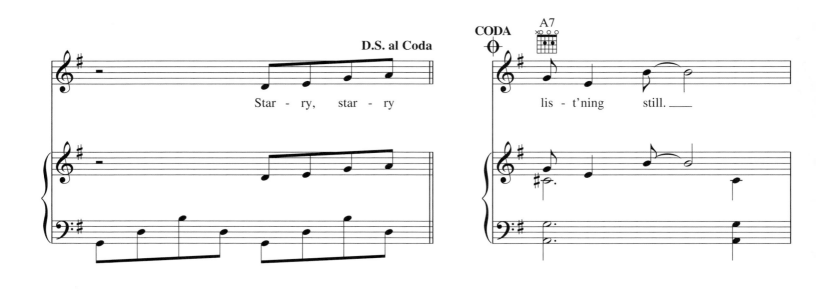

D.S. al Coda

Star - ry, star - ry

CODA

lis - t'ning still. ___

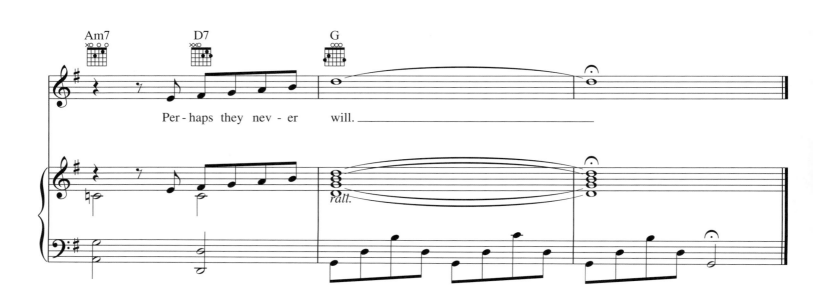

Per - haps they nev - er will. ___

WINTERWOOD

Words and Music by
DON McLEAN

Copyright © 1971, 1972 BENNY BIRD CO., INC.
Copyrights Renewed
All Rights Controlled and Administered by SONGS OF UNIVERSAL, INC.
All Rights Reserved   Used by Permission

There's no place_ I'd_ rath - er be,
They've learned to live_ life_ as they should,

Than at your_ place for the
They're at peace_ with Na - ture's

night.
ways.

No time can pass your sight_ un - seen,
You are as nat - ural as_ the night,

WINTER HAS ME IN ITS GRIP

Words and Music by
DON McLEAN

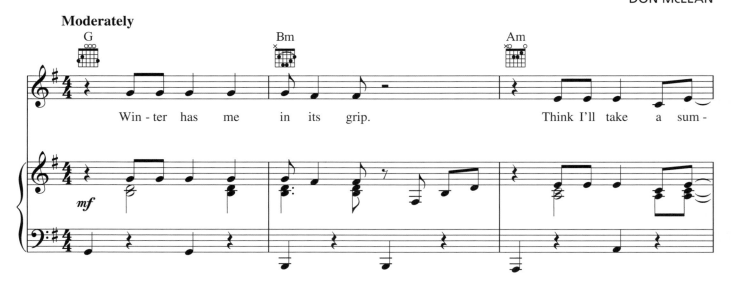

Winter has me in its grip. Think I'll take a sum-

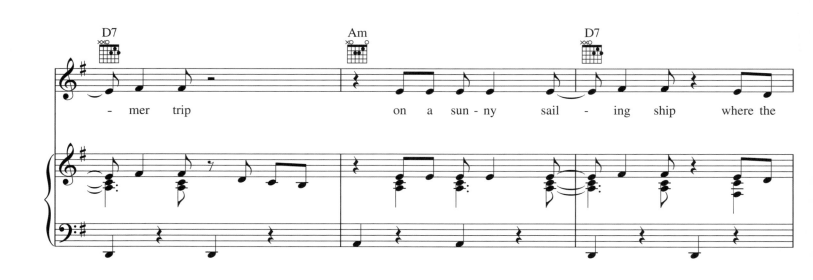

-mer trip on a sun-ny sail-ing ship where the

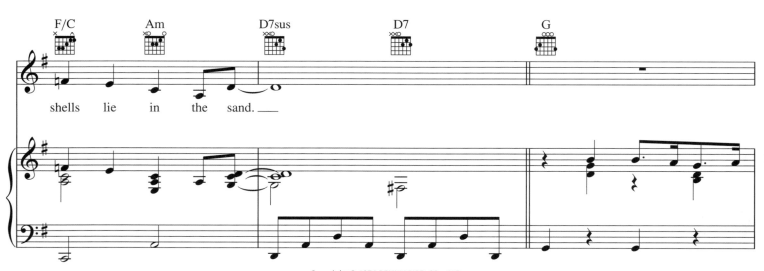

shells lie in the sand. ____

Copyright © 1974 BENNY BIRD CO., INC.
Copyright Renewed
All Rights Controlled and Administered by SONGS OF UNIVERSAL, INC.
All Rights Reserved   Used by Permission

YOU HAVE LIVED

Words and Music by
DON McLEAN

Copyright © 1974 BENNY BIRD CO., INC.
Copyright Renewed
All Rights Controlled and Administered by SONGS OF UNIVERSAL, INC.
All Rights Reserved   Used by Permission

WONDERFUL BABY

Words and Music by
DON McLEAN

Copyright © 1974 BENNY BIRD CO., INC.
Copyright Renewed
All Rights Controlled and Administered by SONGS OF UNIVERSAL, INC.
All Rights Reserved   Used by Permission